In Quest of the Simurgh

SELECTED POEMS BY AHMET MURAT
PREPARED AND COMPILED BY SAMET KOSE

TRAITMARKER BOOKS | FRANKLIN, TENNESSEE

UNITED STATES OF AMERICA

THIS IS A TRAITMARKER BOOK
published in conjunction with
ANDALUCIA PUBLISHING HOUSE

Traitmarker Books
2984 Del Rio Pike
Franklin, TN 37069

ORDERING BOOKS FOR QUANTITY SALES
Special discounts are available on quantity purchases by corporations, associations, and others. For details, contact the author at the address above.

ATTRIBUTIONS
Interior Text Font: Garamond
Editors: Samet Kose & Sharilyn Grayson
Cover Design: Robbie Grayson III

BOOK PUBLISHING INFORMATION
Traitmarker Books
ISBN 978-1-64008-355-4
Published by TRAITMARKER BOOKS
traitmarkerbooks.com
traitmarker@gmail.com

1000 copies ONLY

Printed in the United States of America

CONTENTS

Acclaim

FOR AHMET MURAT

★★★★★

Ahmet Murat's poetry is like hanging on a meta-historic area transcending everyday life. The protagonist sometimes is a child, but most of the time an old saint who is trying to make sense of what's going on around him. His poetry stems from virgin nature, which he views as an explicit theophany. In this sense, he is in close proximity to American poetry. His astonishment at the universe and wonder at nature forces him to build a vertical relationship with the objects. Therefore, a high degree of symbolism and a refined ritualism are evident in his poems. His poetry is a preparation for a ceremony in frenzy and carries the possibility of touching a saint's hands. Ahmet Murat explores the possibility of words that will settle for God's consent.

Harun Tan
Founder and Art Director | Simurg Interdisciplinary Studio

Why do we love Ahmet Murat's poetry? He writes poems like his personality. This provides implicit trust to the reader. In his poems, it's not just people; the life of fruit also exists. We are facing a poet who is looking at nature from a window of wonders and is passionate about trees and birds. This point of view brings forth mercy, kindness, and beauty. Ahmet Murat is writing the highest quality poetry. Sometimes the poems give you peace and comfort; sometimes they make you feel uncomfortable. They give you peace of mind because his poems are crystal clear. They make you feel uncomfortable because they are unequivocally profound. Hence, we have been more cautious when reading his poems. I have followed his poetry for over twenty years. I can say that within his talent, we're in a spacious room overlooking a garden where the air is always fresh.

İbrahim Tenekeci
Poet and Editor | Ketebe Publishing House

Ahmet Murat's poetry is not a poetry passing by but one permanently settled, not a flashing and fading one but one shining constantly, not a poetry of foam but the poetry of water. It brings the past and the future together in the house of the present, into a country with its own time zone, own meridians, and new beginnings and endings. His poems show you the closeness in remoteness and the remoteness in what is close. They are like tulle curtain that imprisons the wind in an unpredictable whiteness and the lasting knowledge that we are temporary ... Ahmet Murat's poetry is a stylistic revolution that embodies abstract wonders like an alchemist. When you enter his poems, you'll notice that what you see is less than what you realize. The bottom line: you hold one of the latest inventions of Turkish and Modern Turkish poetry, which is both ancient and brand new...

Furkan Çalışkan
Poet and Editor | Ketebe Publishing House

Foreword

Ahmet Murat, one of the most important figures in modern Turkish poetry, has proved to be a skilled craftsman in language. He continues a narrative adventure from classical to modern poetry with immaculate Turkish phrasing and robust strings of verses. For these reasons and more, Ahmet Murat is a pioneering Turkish poet.

Ahmet Murat emphasizes and questions methodology and formatting as much as narrative in poetry. For example, *Verdict of the Heart* offers unlimited tastes for poetry readers in terms of technical, aesthetic, and literary pleasure. The characters in Ahmet Murat's poems (such as "Sirto Dance for My Merchant Uncle") are not plain characters, and the characters we think we knew at the beginning of the poem emerge as whole new characters at the end. The places in Ahmet Murat's poetry are also important, and sometimes they even come first from the characters' and poet's point of view. The places are like canvases to a painter. For Ahmet, Rimbaud's escape from modern life, poetry, and fame and his migration to settle in Harar, a walled-city in Africa, are equally fascinating and poetic. For him, creating a good poem as a work of art is an act of expanding the meaning and depth of life and immortalizing what we call life by words, images, and narrative, while at the same time transcending it with a newly-created reality.

Ahmet Murat is one of the few artists who balance formal concerns of poetry in his poems with their sound. He is a master of extracting a sequence of images from a tiny detail, a reluctant look, or a hidden word that ought to be narrated and shared. He exchanges words, creates images, and gives color to his poems, capturing images and associations and opening the doors of consciousness and unconsciousness fully. At the intersection of the first line of one of his poems, one can take an extraordinary journey towards a new destination that even the narrator could not predict. Experiences, testimonies, and observations distill through a profound accumulation of memories and spill out in the forms of strings of words. A promise, a feeling, a situation, an idea, a person, an event, or a resentment is sufficient to inspire a poem. And then, of course, the craftsmanship process starts. Ahmet's mastery in word selection, fluency in construction, ear for sounds, and meticulousness combine in this unique labor. His poems emerge by distilling and brewing. This laborious process reminds me of that brewing and tuning when flute players stand and wait before a dance. This gives us an impression that he has been writing his poems during a prolonged journey. Ahmet Murat is a pioneering poet for accomplishing this goal in a very short period of time.

Important childhood memories and connotations in Ahmet Murat's poetry help us to construe the meaning and significance of destination. As W. H. Auden says, "In the end, all you have is your childhood as your major resources," and "Those children with abundant cool shadows" sadden us when we hear something tragic happened to them. Ahmet Murat stirs those depths, invites us to solve his mysteries, yet remains upbeat, joyful, and hopeful. He presents his poems as a means to counteract what life brings us. His poems in this sense are a mirror, an enthusiasm, a craving, a longing, a peace, a confrontation, a painting, and a journey. He constructs his poetry universe with rhythm, language proficiency, and the richness of the associations within his universe of poetry. He mixes classical forms with newer forms, engaging in an ongoing quest for perfection of form. While reading his poems, you might have a sense of mortal hurt, but those wounds do not stay open. They heal at the end of the poem, corresponding to life as we know it and becoming deeply therapeutic.

A poet master is not a prisoner of reality but the one who constructs the reality. A poet master holds a mirror to the reader, who acquires the reality reflected from the mirror. The poet first and foremost should be careful not merely to reflect life as it is, but to enhance, multiply, and enrich it, hinting at the secrets behind reality. Ahmet Murat meets these expectations by using key concepts and strings of powerful lines. The background of his imagery and the associations it invokes are evident. In this increasingly complex postmodern world, we come across plural identities with multiple selves nested within each other. Ahmet's poems attempt to uncover reality by combining details with whole and seemingly disjointed memories in the minds of his readers. His success as a poet arises from his ability not to produce any kind of imitations for his readers. Despite the presence of all the detailed imagery, the reader feels free to become lost in the streams of Ahmet's thoughts, providing the reader a unique sense of freedom.

In modern Turkish poetry, Ahmet Murat occupies a significant place. Ahmet follows in the footsteps of Anne Bradstreet as he portrays the people living nearby. Ahmet writes about little things: "I wrote about all the little stuff a kid would write about: amazement over things, cats, wounded squirrels found in the street, my friend who moved away, trees, teachers, my funny grandma. I am interested in the personal ramifications of everything, for everybody."

In his first collection of poetry, *Mount Qaf and Its Color*, Ahmet explores the shared experiences and differences between cultures. Ahmet continues this focus in his second collection, *A Poet on a Bike*, writing about ordinary life and the perspectives of people in other lands as a record of an essentially lost or forgotten world. Ahmet creates poetry from everyday scenes, celebrating the similarities between us all, as well as our differences and diversity. Ahmet's third collection of poetry, *Winter Knowledge*, reflects a new but more mature perspective, influenced by the continuing unrest in our lives and the tragedy and sorrow present there. Still, Ahmet maintains an undertone of hope, realizing that facing sorrow and adversity does not kill us but only makes us stronger.

Ahmet's most recent poetry book, *Verdict of the Heart*, is full of his finest work in terms of imagery and style. He invites the reader to take a dreamlike journey amid orange trains and dusty stations, lonely squirrels, plums and almonds, olives, sprouts, capricorns, resentful jonquils, acacias, pheasants, goats and gazelles, dervish lodges and fuqaras, barefooted majzoobs, exhausted monks, sandalwood fragrances, bundles of mint, cheesecloths, caravans, merchants, and bedouins, all spiraling into a turquoise voyage. With influences from Mahmoud Darwish to Arthur Rimbaud, Ahmet's poems stand as a masterpiece awaiting keen poetry lovers.

I found Ahmet Murat's poems for the first time through a dear common friend. When I read *Verdict of the Heart*, I felt the pleasant stab of truth and the presence of divinity. So I have woven *In Quest of the Simurgh* with genuine, heartfelt blessings, hoping to reach Western poetry readers with the same sense of enlightenment and to offer these images to their hearts and minds. I send my sincere good wishes to Ahmet Murat, whom I trust will continue to write many more profound and sophisticated poems, touching hearts and minds thousands of miles away from him.

SAMET KOSE
FRANKLIN, TENNESSEE
OCTOBER 31, 2018

SELECTED POEMS

Mount Qaf and Its Color

ONE THING REMAINS

I praise your observation of the land and sea
remote cheers of elder sisters dancing
with the last warming of water and earth
a child applauds an orange train
people remember this when they see you now.

People remember this when they see you now
I remember, too, but slowly, gently
sated horses in the barns, deepen the fullness of night
then I forget about it, forget the rest
they are already embedded in memories,
        I will bury them again
as if I were a child, a patient, and a sea
a lonely squirrel obviously
resented his buried nuts.

We split it up: you go North!
if you want, I can share my horse with you
take some water, fruit, and matches
the bloodshed waiting for a ballad,
but don't forget the sounds we rinsed clear

THEODICY[1]

Like one of the first people's eyes
my eyes were clashing with the geometry of the night
a pair of black scales: weighing starlight
            and a ferment of twitters,
at the floor where angels cracked their wings
when it falls down
it falls from there in between us.

Between us there is a chamber of admiration
we rested three days off that wood-core fruit
and why do insects fail to get there
while touching to start a family
and bleeding to each other?
Our faith to plums and almonds is complete
his presence pleasing children's mouths,
young mice, even moles go down with him
to the amusement park of living roots.

We must see in sudden appearances
if someone seems two to you, seems one to me
on the base of a mountain or an underground river
the fish net old lovers braided together patiently
from each other's hairs should hit me in the face
and should retreat following the school of fish.

You're an alchemist; see how I deduced the truth
from your white coat smelling of chemicals,
        medicines flowing in our midst
and love: industrious inside, replenishing
my armour of foams and burns.

------

[1]*The term* theodicy *was coined by German philosopher Gottfried Leibniz in his 1710 work, written in French,* Essais de Théodicée sur la Bonté de Dieu, La Liberté de L'homme et L'origine du Mal *(Theodicy: Essays on the Goodness of God, the Freedom of Man and the Origin of Evil). Theodicy literally means justifying God's will and actions.*

*(*For further explanation, see the extensive note on the last page).*

A RANGE NAMED REMOTE

Heralded by the lost stars
let it emerge at the longest evening
the most rainful of my loved ones

Songs soothing the passengers
are at my heart with broken lips
they call it sofra[2], central place, but we can't stay here
as the bubbling weddings fade away

In dusty stations, sleepy domes,
my throat, a basket of ashes, holds the remains of my voice
the silent sacred scripts on my forehead
speak to the women whose children slipped into heaven
instead of their arms

____

[2]_sofra: the low table around which a family eats together in Turkish
culture_

PRAISE TO THE SPUR
FOR THE FUQUARA[3]

This time of year
my silence keeps all crossings with its liquor
sparrow feathers softly inside
sea snakes are flowing like an underwater call for prayer.
freshly washed face of awareness
the undoubted tray of unusual berries
broken with joy from rare stones, lightful teeth

Dear sheikh, our hands are like a dove
        stretched on the branches,
they respectfully remembered an ancient
        stringed instrument,
we've built a prayer that was on the floor
gorgeous eyes of awareness seen in our eyes

I apologize for all those abandoned wirds[4]
from all women indecently drunk, from water
it will be warm like a morning bread
let our mouths break down behind those prayers

---

[3]*fuqara: an Arabic word which can mean either the poor generally or Sufi dervishes specifically*
[4]*wird: daily prayer of Sufis*

MOUNT QAF[5] AND ITS COLOR

When sleep pulls the ladder for the last time
let my scream cease and stare up in the air,
that tumor in my chest will be a bubbling wreath
while I was falling down to crash.

The night dozes off, reaching the ragged summers
the epigraph inside me from a mountain and the sea,
they made my travel music by colliding
those horses gathered in a unique darkness.

The old man whom the serpents know and the brown color
and imaginary math - cannot get out of the gardens -
this is well, and the upcoming tremble should find me ready
while the angel was erring with the rifle of death.

---

[5]*Mount Qaf in Arabian cosmology is a mysterious mountain of ancient Muslim tradition renowned as the "farthest point of the earth" owing to its location at the far side of the ocean encircling the earth. This mythical mountain is mentioned in two novels by Salman Rushdie: Grimus and Shame. Mount Qaf (the original Turkish title is Kafdağı) is also the title of a novel by Turkish author Müge İplikçi.*

THE BALLAD OF MILITARY MOBILIZATION

The Spring is progressive with its ploughshare feet
red flows through a cherry tree, some of us to the song,
the masculinity surging through the bulls and stallions
support water's ambition of floating.
The woman is the restless fingers of the plain
changing the flurry of flowers, wherever they are
the glasses of music in the borders of the field
the theater of bulghur wheat, edible music of the peasants.

My hands, my feet, my body
handless footless animals are waking up.
The spinning wheels are waking up at the poplar trees,
biceps of the angels: smoky bowls going up and down,
a partisan reciting mountain names with dire respect
while sprouts were rustling to his vessels
and with respect to the big drums of bridge free wild vessels
while the partisan sees the lake and
wishes to skip some flat stones.

Then you unplug a piece of rock (you can unplug)
you know you dump the dirt with your finger (you)
you know, even if I did not say
you thought it with your index finger
and flying and fighting for a favor

little noises of flower dusts
maybe even the missing shadows
motherhood boiling down while a mother
          breastfeeds her child
I am that sail boat now blowing and not blowing those winds.

If I rip that hand now
kissing my lips for a noon necklace,
blowing some animal horns to make men soldiers
issuing a freshly strangled capricorn inside each one.

A Poet on a Bike

POEM OF A HESITATION

Dear diary, I am tired this Sunday
I took tests on social studies and religion last night
studied real art, full all the way down my throat
with great music, long novels, and immaculate pride
I changed my skin while zipping through Beşiktaş[6]
It's Sunday; I'm going to take Sunday papers today
pressing them to my wounds with their supplements
to the petite bourgeoisie, a block of pods
    the balcony pleases me with begonias and more
knowing that ferryboats are passing by ceaselessly.

Happy Sunday ice creams are melting,
        and the fish are smolting
you hear that, dear diary?
I'm stepping down at the first stop while pouring lyrics
potato print chicks are stepping down as well, oh master
mascaras, pimples, positive energies are stepping down
on my head sits a moon from my best lines
on the way out grasping an urban distress
grandiose, voluminous.

Nuclear families rub weekdays together
with worries, installments, the middle girl's crushes
we should take the kids to the beach,
        people should look like each other

ships passing far away, my teenage years
I should say, father, I see a mask from smoke on your face
mother should say in her sleep, I'm afraid
let the ships sail far away for many years.

The sea blinds their eyes, kids
kids are on the brink of a breaking fast
and the sea is a glare in the city's teeth,
and the sea is Eve awakened with salt.

____

⁶*Beşiktaş: a district of Istanbul*

A POET ON A BIKE

While the green grasses are weighing the wind in the plains
we were looking out at a rain bus
a young man startled and passed by the hill
we thought that hill has changed
or we thought, that hill has changed.

Something happened, and the coffees cast with the first love
got cold, and a tired bird died
a pot dried out, and a caterpillar was despised
everybody inquired: what was that, what was that
as if a big sip silenced our insides.

A poet on a bike was riding through green grasses,
that hill, a rain, a poem, and a late afternoon altogether
winding to the right and to the left,
in fact nothing there to hit, while passing through.

TRAFFIC

You should find a name to this play we put on stage
I say anonymous on the stage, anonymous on the stage
you're saying fate is such a rich word
when I say a train warms up another train
you say I hear a whip of a cloud on my face
you say fountains are left open and the
          spring is about to burst.

You say this world is huge for a game but for a game of two
it appears tiny for a moment in my eye for some reason
don't tell anyone but the arrival was a farewell
they raised me with Atay[7] and Dosto[8]
they're all mixed with my blood from
          whatever direction they blow
they burned and incensed me with letters in this game

I'm saying that there is such a thing as under this tree
listen to what I have to say about this under tree
the trees die in adulthood with lightning
whether this world is tiny or huge
your solid heart or soft mind.

Do you have some change in the meantime?
I have to go home; something bad happened
I have to go to the market, too,

in order to enter the line of making payments
I have to hurry also
but I can't say this about this game
in this life we always had a thing called under tree

If the world would not lead to talking about it
there would not be such a thing named game in my life
I would keep the conversation when it
comes to about the world
    you know all the way till country
this is not a good place to raise a family
and moreover traffic is preventing talking about the world
and the poetry.

---

[7]*Atay is Oğuz Atay (1934–1977), a pioneer of the modern novel in Turkey. His first novel, Tutunamayanlar (The Disconnected), appeared in 1971-72. Never reprinted in his lifetime and controversial among critics, it has become a best-seller since a new edition came out in 1984. It has been described as "probably the most eminent novel of twentieth-century Turkish literature."*
[8]*Dosto refers to Fyodor Mikhailovich Dostoyevsky (1821–1881), Russian novelist, short story writer, essayist, journalist, and philosopher. Dostoyevsky's literary works explore human psychology in the troubled political, social, and spiritual atmosphere of 19th-century Russia and engage with a variety of philosophical and religious themes. The poet uses an abbreviated version of Dostoyevsky's name, Dosto, which is close to the word for companion in Turkish.*

PREPARATIONS FOR SPRING IN PALESTINE
WITH ELEMENTS BORROWED FROM MAHMOUD DARWISH'S POEMS

A doe is departing between orange blossoms
as if she listened to pieces of poetry from Davut[9],

The big olives are swelling at the disturbance
        of approaching girls
a dog is licking the scars of the holy lands

The creek is stirring with the sound of ancient poets
a creek, in honor of the friendships
        of the children who gathered
    thyme
Oh our home's bread, you're like Arabic poetry,
        burning and hard
while the people in exile were feeding on
        tuberculosis and nostalgia

Aunt date is not casting a shadow yet,
        offending jonquil and pods
and mothers are digging dirty laundry from the ground

The elderly are pulling their callous tasbihs[10]: lâ hawla[11]
the roots of dead children are raising the ground

---

[9]*The Prophet Davut (also David or Davud) is mentioned in both Mus-*

lim and Christian sacred texts
[10]*tasbih: a short, repetitive prayer glorifying the name of Allah.*
[11]*lâ hawla: the beginning of a well-known tasbih meaning "there is no power or strength except through Allah."*

A DERVISH[12] LODGE DIARY

An abdal[13] is milking those tits of jins[14]
around their eyes a stardust mascara.
The sounds and dreams of a chorus of forty at sunrise,
ceasing their sleep in bed like slicing a cheese,
their smokeless flaming voices simmering a prayer,
a prayer: like a dried plum softened
          on the first prophet's tongue
a prayer: neither soft nor hard
but an aniseed anguish rising into the air.

A goat got lost at the mountain trail
a tune in its tongue, the sound of a cloud soaked in static
a sleep-deprived pin in night's hand grenade
a tailor's hand touched her, stitching the nerves vertically
a goat gazes upwards
ancestral verses viscous in her blood
digging flower wells with fingernails
with sandalwood fragrance emanating from the lodge
sharpening the memory of her fingernails.

They are pulling the morning prayers from the well
invisible waterlilies sleeping in ice-cold water
waterlilies reminiscent of virgin mothers.
The water wounds their hands like looming puberty
dervishes; their mouths are one oven,

oscillating with Ism-i Celal[15]
their mouths are leaking honey,
        cracked with massive hidden secrets
their bodies turn like pages riffling in the morning wind[16].

A city is breathing on their rib cages
a book is erasing itself, a peacock gets sweaty
a new day is beginning as if torn apart from the ancient world
blushing like an apple severed from Heaven.

----

[12]*dervish: a Sufi ascetic who uses physical motion or exertion to reach a state of devotion to God*
[13]*abdal: (the word means substitute) refers sometimes to a rank of forty saints, but more often to a group of 356 saints in the Sufi sect that only Allah knows and chooses. Their actions keep the world going. The word can also apply in a larger sense to saints in general.*
[14]*Jins are the same beings known in English as genies; the Quran uses the term jin.*
[15]*Ism-i celal: a kind of dervish recital, usually performed while seated on the knees. In many dervish lodges (tekkes) they were performed every morning after morning prayer and formed part of the morning service. The term means "Almighty Lord's Name."*
[16]*"The morning wind spreads its fresh smell. We must get up and take that in, that wind that lets us live. Breathe before it's gone." Rumi*

Winter Knowledge

A SERMON IN THE FOREST

Sometimes I tell myself I've found you
while taking the fish nets out of the water
you will find water like me
I looked at you once and saw clouds and drums
kids you took in your poems and afternoons
in which I made cold water for the horses.

They say the forest is large and dark,
        and insects are feverish - so what?
Moving away from you strengthens me to pursue you
I whistle the tune; the forest road gives me happiness
I listen to my chest while passing through the thorns
and cherish gazing at gazelles pushing
        wild fruit with their noses in the same line.

What's in there that I find you
you're chewing a daphne leaf or something it resembles
you start a new rain when one ceases
you are gorgeous and courteous and created from clay.

COUNTED LINES FINISH EARLY[17]

This poem is my second of today
I finished the first, then lost my desire
darling, I can recite it; why do you stand there like a stranger?
It was supposed to be a tercet, so to speak.

Started the second stanza with seven words -
you counted seven; now you're not my beloved
but I still need to finish this poem; hopefully I will finish
we can still be friends, though I do not prefer that.

A cloud is moving inside me, a sip
a line, a mind, a reminiscence of companionship
a progress, the loud joy of an avalanche from the North,
and darling, to underline the end of the poem.
It's finished now.

---

[17]*There is a Turkish saying used to comfort the hearer, "counted lines finish early," that people use when saying farewell to a soldier leaving his family to fulfill a mandatory military service or to someone going to jail. Here, counted lines (verses) of a poem finish early.*

WINTER KNOWLEDGE

Winters are full of wolves like smoke
a powerful breath checks a couple of pines
chimneys exude the gloominess of a youth
who remembers his father, or anything meaningful
in the boarding house.

A person should look at another in the winter,
seek his gaze refined through a cheesecloth
made of snow and mist a few nights
as if he understand the stones
falling to the remote lakes in darkness.

The plant roots in icy creeks
slow their breathing as they enter their dreams
tire tracks in the snow are leading to Dostoyevsky
visible in the snow then invisible
is the horse of a life span.

BESIDES

I write poems about seasons, this and that
some yellows tend towards a passionate naiveté
or a spring finds itself standing
as the host of a wedding
a bird is resurrecting the plains as if pumping them gas
while passing through the sunrise with pensive thoughts.

A pheasant blooms out of the warehouses and coals
in the name of October or November among the months,
as long as boarding schoolers are pursuing
          new raging poems
over there among the rains and Saturdays.
Far away: books multiply
far away: a bunch of grapes glittering
far away: a form warms and chills by turns
far away: a force transforms everything
          I wrote for the seasons
a resin of anxiety, a swirling dark resin waits far away.

SIRTO DANCE FOR MY MERCHANT UNCLE

It looks like a mill awakening
grinding down the grain, the stalk

Scales are rising and waking
chubby cats of sack tops

A man down the hill and his hunger:
merchants' morning, morning is for merchants

Geraniums decorate balconies, and sleep decorates children
merchants' morning extinguishes like a lamp
        the bodies of dogs barking in the distance

If the great hunger of humanity would not find soothing
in batiste, in limestone, and silver

It spins its shadow in the market in a few seconds
consciousness expands like steam within a hot loaf of bread
endears itself to Rimbaud[18] in Harar[19]
merchants' morning

____

[18]*Arthur Rimbaud (1854-1891) was a French poet who produced his best known works while still in his late teen years but gave up creative writing altogether before the age of 20. Victor Hugo described him at the time as "an infant Shakespeare." As part of the decadent movement, Rimbaud influenced modern literature, music and art. His poem*

"Voyelles" invoked synesthesia, marking him as a founder of French symbolism, and his "Une Saison en Enfer" (A Season in Hell) is considered one of the first works of free verse. He was known to have been a libertine and a restless soul, travelling extensively on three continents before his death from cancer just after his 37th birthday. Rimbaud's life and poetry have inspired a great number of poets and artists, including the French symbolists, Surrealism, the counter-culture Beat movement, and the musicians Bob Dylan, Jim Morrison, and Patti Smith.

[19]Harar: a walled city in Eastern Ethiopia. In December of 1880, Arthur Rimbaud entered the ancient walled city of Harar, Ethiopia, a journey that had involved crossing the Gulf of Aden in a wooden dhow and 20 days on horseback through the Somali Desert. Harar was a market town threaded with steep cobblestone alleys that wind between high limestone and tuff walls. Today those walls are painted with geometric designs in green, white, pink, and blue. As one strolls down the narrow, mazelike streets lined with single-story dwellings, the city, fortified and enigmatic, feels closed off. Harar is surrounded by walls built between the 13th and 16th centuries, with several main gates. In the densely populated Old City, there are over 180 mosques and shrines, some dating to the 10th century. Harar had been a Sufi Muslim center of learning closed to outsiders for hundreds of years before the explorer Sir Richard Burton entered the city in 1855. The adventurous Rimbaud immediately recognized Harar as an intriguing business prospect at the edge of the known world. The Arthur Rimbaud Cultural Center opened in 2000 to credit Rimbaud, who loved Harar and Hararis and who preferred Harar to his sophisticated, nationalized Europe and wanted to die in Harar. Rimbaud highlighted the risks and difficulties of his life in Africa in letters to his disapproving mother. "This last expedition has exhausted me so much that I often lie in the sun, immobile like an unfeeling stone," he wrote. Another trip he described as "insane cavalcades through the steep mountains of the country." Rimbaud declared, "I loved desert, scorched orchards, sun-bleached shops, warm drinks. I dragged myself through stinking streets and, eyes closed, offered myself to the sun, god of fire." In November 1891, at 37, Arthur Rimbaud died while dictating a note to the director of the Messageries Maritimes shipping line. "Let me know what time I shall be carried on board," he

*requested in his letter. Until the end, the brilliant polymath was deter-
mined to return to the city where he had finally found a kind of peace.*

JUST ME

The day is dismissed by these pine tips, this bundle of mints,
the bubbling pot in the balcony, the smell of milk inside,
a gentle weight on my shoulder, a friend's hand,
what else hushes this world?
A sweet weight on top of me, the shadow of a bird,
that I buried inside my forgotten story
wakes up, wakes up gently the silver mole and its clock.

I say immediately, youth is a branch angling inside me
rest assured, a single cloud is left to be teased.
I ask the place where seasons rub against each other -
        just in time
these bird feathers, moth-wing powders
if seasons do not rub against each other, well, then why?

What's that, heard after a prayer for rain?
Blood opens my veins thinking about it,
knocks on the door, really as if I have a door
knocks again like a heart from one of the seven sleepers[20].
That sound slows down the hectic prayers suddenly
breaks down pearly, immaculate fingernails,
and withers greedy young directors, such a sound
brings forth a whole new milk from an animal
            never seen before
life of a fruit, temperament of the sea, human voice

it would welcome itself in amazement if returned.
It drifts into the children's awakening like snow
passing through their sleep like a plow
the clouds of their soul inflate
and mothers would only consider the fate.

This is it: a mind, a spark, the work of a man,
a couple of dreams jump suddenly inside me
as if the apple stands up from the sap inside the tree.
rustles as deep as silk
when it's morning with birds
pulling a night-warm blanket over me.

The sky opens up like a new lesson
from a gazelle's skin and two wings from the Surah Al-Asr[21],
childhood created and demolished
        in the inside rooms of big houses
replicates joy like breaking beans
the scale of an unfinished poem moves.

Continents, islands ... I sail away with it, with it
and a poem calls down an avalanche,
an eternal alchemy lesson for every poetry filling.
I think I can gather some speed then in those
        races towards mothers,
I feel like I'm going to overtake the sea foam
and I guess I'll save the docks from losing the mists.

---

[20]*Seven Sleepers: The story of the companions of the cave is found in the 18th surah of the Quran, al-Kahf (the Cave), for which the surah is*

named. It relates the tale of a young group of believers who fall into a supernatural sleep in a cave, only to awaken hundreds of years later. This story mimics a story found in the Syriac homily by a Christian bishop named Jacob of Serugh (521 CE). His story tells of seven young Christians in Ephesus (an ancient Greek city now situated in modern-day Turkey), who hide from an evil emperor in a cave, fall into a supernatural sleep for hundreds of years, and awaken to find that their hometown has been converted to Christianity.

[21]*Surah Al-Asr (The Time): This Surah takes its name from the word "al-`asr" occurring in the first verse. This Surah has 3 verses (100: 1-3) in the Quran. "By time. The human being is in loss. Except those who believe, and do good works, and encourage truth, and recommend patience."*

A LONELY WOMAN DANCING

Borges[22] dances tango, the blind Jorge Luis
smells the woman whose hands shaped cheese
distracted by the books
he cannot see anyone
a taste saddens the woman; she never knew it before

The equator extends from open windows quietly
crushing oranges endlessly in its path
Bor-ges! Bor-ges!
The entire hall stands
to wake him with applause.

____

[22]*Jorge Luis Borges (1899–1986): Argentine author Jorge Luis Borges ex-
erted a strong influence on the direction of literary fiction through his
genre-bending metafictions, essays, and poetry. Borges was a founder
and principal practitioner of postmodernist literature, a movement in
which literature distances itself from life situations in favor of reflection
on the creative process and critical self-examination. Widely read and
profoundly erudite, Borges was a polymath who could discourse on
the great literature of Europe and America and who assisted his trans-
lators as they brought his work into different languages. Borges's work
"constitutes, through his extreme linguistic conscience and a formal
synthesis capable of representing the most varied ideas, an instance
of supreme development in and renovation of narrative techniques.
With his exemplary literary advances and the reflective sharpness of his
metaliterature, he has effectively influenced the destiny of literature."*

Verdict
of
the Heart

VERDICT OF THE HEART

First left, then right, left again
the mind turns, the heart ceases to prolong
the mind knows two times two thoroughly
the heart will deny two's existence.

People are asleep; they wake when they die[23],
he is the man of the day and welcomed aboard.
The soul wakes up; tis the time for the heart's verdict:
God may surprise you, the Lord of the realms.

The mind weighs the verdict of the heart
reminiscent of this: the mind is a merchant
reminiscent of that: the mind gets wounded
the heart never gets wounded; it is the wound itself.

---

[23]*"People are asleep; when they die they will wake up." - Prophet Muhammad*

ON THE ROAD

Darling, I owe you a long journey,
but love shortens all roads.
These curves twist to meet fate,
close your eyes; the chill seeps inside!

If you're on a long journey, take my word - return!
Acacias, rivers, and cicadas,
they all murmur the same verse:
He is closer to you than your jugular vein[24].

We live a lie in the time of speed; so pick up your pace,
if you cannot escape from the world you're unhurried,
the road whispers to you, words dissolve in there,
fever in horses and spirited stars.

------

[24]*Refers to a verse in Quran (50:16):*
"We created the human being, and We
know what his soul whispers to him. We
are nearer to him than his jugular vein."

A DEFENSE IN-DEPTH

Tears are agents of God.
Praising them is a sacred art.
Among the two people which
dry, but not perished, are tears.

Tears flow and tell you - what?
Or are they the Archangel's sweat?
They ferment a lover's heart,
as if God gazed upon those tears.

Tears, thirty-two obligations[25], and the Ilmihal[26].
Now I look at a poet's sleeplessness,
elusive tears in the heart of a poet.
Tears are not the work of God's servants.

---

[25]32 obligations: 6 pillars of faith, 5 pillars of Islam, 12 obligatory acts of prayer (salah), 4 of minor ablution (Wudhu), 3 of major ablution (Ghusl), 2 of ablution with sand or earth (tayammum), for a total of 32.
[26]Ilmihal (Catechism): A concise book in which Muslims may find teachings of Islam, principles of faith, and basic religious practical information which is essential in their daily lives.

LOOK OF THOSE LEFT BEHIND

Emre's sister was dead, Ziya's sweetheart, Nazan's soulmate,
those left behind are looking among
          the oriental sweetgum trees
a half-earthling, humanized with the taste of a fruit
half-divine.

They're going to overcome,
a darkness impressed on their looks,
and they're looking different from yesterday, and past years,
they're looking at the darkness of a winter white.

Their gaze gave them, they already became someone else,
it's a lie what they say; you cannot die with the dead.

SOMETIMES A LATE AFTERNOON

The sea was caressing the coast with boats
plants piled up; so did early morning hours,
children's sounds like lightning lemons
bounce from one house to another.

I was there to be forgotten; so was the train station courtyard
sorrows and joys were judging me,
a pool at the center, an Elvan Gazoz[27], and Neşe Karaböcek[28]
sometimes a late afternoon was swirling sparrows.

It's hard to believe that summer is ending
it's hard to believe that summer is ending
I'd change by repeating this sentence
my blue and white shirts.

---

[27]*Elvan Gazoz: a famous soda in Turkey back in the poet's childhood years*
[28]*Neşe Karaböcek (1947–): a Turkish singer who is considered one of the main artists of Turkish Arabesque music, a fusion of traditional Turkish and world music influences and adaptations of international sounds. She also starred in a great number of Turkish films. She was awarded multiple gold and platinum certifications.*

OUTSIDE TODAY

I have a music inside me, floating with content,
who put that all the way over there, who?
I traveled with it throughout the day; it got tired, too
you could listen to it, and you liked it.

I saw us in an old picture today
it seemed like we forgot about the two of them there,
our hands were naive; our eyes were wiser
and we were so young - stop crying.

I have some questions; certainly I have,
for example - is love a form of satiety or hunger?
For example - what if I say, do you believe in freedom,
when absorbed with this much love, still?

LAST SERMON

Dear congregation! I fear God, but I'm terrified of heights
this minbar[29] has so many steps - hey, you in the front
say, if it wasn't for my fear of heights, perhaps I'd ascend
I'd fly two glasses, with a denial,
          and a song from the minaret.

Congregation! Let them make an escalating minbar[30]
in Dubai and a Heaven simulator - to be prepared
The Religious Affairs Directorate renewed the language of
     religion; he is a new one
La hawla wa la quwwata, La hawla wa la quwwata[31].

Oh Dear! I was afraid of heights, but don't you be afraid
God is not as you know, but I am
I'd fly, monthly bills, beards in my face, and you,
          my dears, around
I'd fly, if you'd said from the beginning that you were a lie.

---

[29]*minbar: a pulpit in the mosque where the imam (prayer leader) stands to deliver sermons or in the Hussainia where the speaker sits and lectures the congregation. The word is a derivative of the Arabic root n-b-r ("to raise, elevate"); the Arabic plural is manābir.*
[30]*minaret: a tall tower from the top of which prayers are called.*
[31]*La hawla wa la quwwata: "There is no power and no strength save in Allah."*

DARLING

I'm your life out there
the meaning of your life, drift of its meaning, this and that
my two arms, strong shoulders, my life and death
we are both sad that I just mentioned death;
        let's not make each other sad
let's just say, oh death, our names crunch
        a cigarette in your mouth
oh death, your drums populate households
you're a phosphorous syrup at Adam's table
darling, you're like that when you divide us
I'm your life, you long to see me in the evening and morning
it is a puzzle to me your unraveling the days
        and weaving them
evening morning evening morning evening morning.

I'm the base of your life, the bandsaw and Big Brother
the reason you like a flower and a reason to light a fire
the format of pouring into a flower, your declining
        to discuss a flower
I'm your life: so declares the Holy Scripts, poems,
        and poet sultans.
You want to whistle and occupy a window if I'm gone
to see water in glass and to drink a storm in a glass of water
I bring life to them, I know them, they're fine
a nightmare in your life, I lumber along

if our sentences are raw, unrefined, I am a delusion,
and you are no one.
I am your life, a quiet life in khaki
do I look similar to someone else? No, No, Yes
my quietness compiles the life stories of unplucked vines
a penetrating sleep in logic lectures - that's me.

To love me, to run towards me, to take years off me
to add a music to you, then to listen to you
declare a war to cast lots to shed some beards
        to curl a moustache
to like kebab rent a house to keep a household
        to spend summer in the highlands
these turn like a tasbih between you and me
dealings of the life caravan of alimonies, subsistence,
        and garbage disposal tax
God's gift is children and the children's gift is tenderness
these are like a tasbih[32] between you and me
while we are two bricks cooked in social sciences
        juxtaposed side-by-side.

I'm your life, your I love you - who can appeal to this?
Your honor, common sense, or American public opinion?
The findings are sufficient, consciousness is calm,
        and awareness is content
I'm covering your life with mine, no! (my) woman no cry

A human is a remote thing and island man, well
talking is a delusion; words are huge, possibly
who isolates who; who forwards who;

and what is so-called who
a human being is side-by-side with another, what's this, alas,
        who's going to believe this?
But I'm your life, negator of philosophy,
        affirmative with poetry
spilling out from force to the verb, from surface to the core
'tis time to eliminate the evidence of a
        public departure wound
your committed listening is scaling water
        to the words of steel
your flags are adorning poetry, loosening the stitches of a
dark coma.

---

[32]*tasbih: a Muslim's prayer beads*

A SPECIAL PRAYER

God, can I talk to you? I beg your forgiveness
you are talking to me, but I cannot hear - oh please forgive
I talked a lot, mostly empty talk; I filled in the blanks
I have alienated myself, like a half glass of tea
you put sugar in me, though, I didn't taste sweet
I couldn't understand you in t-shirt messages, street names,
plate letters - I was hopeful from all;
          I got stuck with a compact consciousness,
I couldn't understand the rains, got cold in the snow,
      you know
I am a fan of umbrellas, unlike those frivolous
          mysterious poetry lovers
I got headaches in Southwest winds;
          you know I have sinusitis,
      and I'm allergic to the rain
You made a poet of me; that's your strength.
          If I ask if you are content
it helps me to speak to you; I'm very happy.

I liked words, foreign words, even hostile ones
some had a cinnamon smell, some were dried like a date,
          some blew a chrysanthemum
I kept them all inside, even though I let them arise
          to the sky like a chicory.

I look at the sky like a bedouin, illiterate, cheerful -
        God is in heaven,
you wrote the sky; I couldn't read it,
        a resin taste in my tongue
in my mind, heart, and thoughts, a place in my heart,
        wishful for the lily of your beauty.
God, you know me; have you written a happy ending for me?
    please share with your servant
I forgot some of my lines; I stole some roles,
        dozed off on the stage
but now - here came the good news and a gift
I have words I did not use, saved and blinded when uttered
pulled them through the lost languages,
        from the dialects of the blind hafiz[33]
pooled words for this morning's attack from the
        national anthems,
memoirs of forgotten dervishes, from the notes of
        mediocre scholars,
memorization of the ones unable to love,
        from the notebooks of unread authors,
I collected all those words; I sat on the gambling table
I've got the world's most bizarre hand.
        My luck is ignited from one end, I can see
I'm here on the brink of sinking, please destroy me,
        assign me for destruction
do not let me bypass the rivers,
        push me from the rafts, put me into seclusion
so that neither the black nor the white of my eyes
        slips into any one else but you.

Prophet Moses[34] comes to my mind;
        you talked forty days with him
lofty words, stark commands, and full exclamations
a malaria fever breathed forty days at the mountain steps
a ballad mixed the figs with honey, and incensed the thymes
the Earth perpetually trembled with the spear of your speech
I'd love to have heard Prophet Moses coming
        down from the mountain
first words from that stutter, heavenly language to smooth
that stutter, from the language he refused
I'd love to see his eyes, cured from wine the past forty days
his voice brewed with noble worries, eyes departed
        from the beloved
I'd love to kiss his hands, bending like two
        willow branches from the sky
you talked with him, seasoned him with the salt
        of an utterance
you let electric fishes flow from his tongue,
        then history flowed
filled with inception, with no way to escape from you
it's good news that there is no escape from you,
        great news, and the latest news
I'm falling into your arms like falling asleep after a sleep.
He's the face of your name in any language, some of them
        familiar, some burning with glory
your names cut letters like lightning
crossed lines, dazzled mouths, it's as if you arrived
it's not Turkish, not Turkish, not Aramaic either
remnants from the language of scriptures,
        some prophet dialects

from the Mediterranean Sea
whispered hidden names like the winds that fill the galleons
sediments from the glory that interrupts the sleep of snakes
last exhalation of an exhausted monk
        embracing the keys of an organ
while the sounds of the grapes grow pale
a cave in my chest collects them all
to all the big caves, to all reticent reclusives, to all
saints settled on the mountains, all had ordeals,
        and all rest content
my cave is opening to all caves they nested
the smell of sandal trees in my nose,
        the deer skin they wrapped around
the smell of bread they couldn't eat,
        the smell of the mouth of a fasting man
I hold it all inside me, in order to choose
        a language from languages
so that my breath can suffice for all of your names,
        hence, therefore.

I'm going to go read these verses at the orifice of mountains
on the edge of a creek, I will collect the fish near me
hyacinths will bow to hear your name
the creek perhaps will squirm downstream
as if I am a poet; we'll see if I am
if I can get a great blend of grief and hope
then I am a poet, I guess, when intellect
        and transcendence nest together
when caterpillars of your love move inside
        the cocoon of your heart.

A daydream passes through songs,
        drawing blood from the radio
a singer's voice breaks like a pretzel, I hear
urgently I want to fight with life in the same highway
to tear off the seat belt, to race past the speed limit,
        cool bare head, hot bare feet
but the daydream in those songs stops me,
ends me, problems knot my joints
last days of autumn clot inside my joints, suddenly
yellow leaves are bitter, even bitter for a poor street sweeper
I want a space where these seasons cease
a dull, numb, timeless space
only a place where your name hangs like a remote star
a dark plain resonates with your name in my forties
oh, my beloved students celebrating my prophetic age
        with cake and latte,
how do you do?
I could hear your verses from open windows in Fez[35]
those verses restoring the city each morning
prophet names flew through the streets at dawn
the angels have landed, we choked Pharaoh,
        we're in sacred paths, holy scriptures in our hands
chewing gums from olive leaves in our mouths,
        here we come, wonderful on camels
tour verses burning streets like fireworks - Allahu Akbar[36]
it looks like we're back to the primal human,
        ready to fight with our nafs[37]

I think, we buried majzoobs[38], they were cruising
        like a bomb in those markets
like a pause in life, they were pushing life towards life.

I keep comforting myself, you have no idea (you know)
I keep reading stories of lovers, I believe in all those lunatics
each one of them, quiet, full of pensive thoughts
you stole them from their large tents, small tents
when their tongues moved vaguely, the pearls of your names
        went bouncing on the floor
as if they shared memories with you, but they hid it - why?
I can't interfere, I guess, and I can't go back either,
oh, where do I belong, oh the owner of selves,
        oh the owner of whereabouts!

---

[33]*hafiz: one who has memorized the Quran*
[34]*Moses: The Prophet Moses appears in both Muslim and Christian sacred texts.*
[35]*Fez: the second largest city in Morocco, as well as its capital until 1925*
[36]*Allahu Akbar: God is great.*
[37]*nafs: equivalent of self in Sufism*
[38]*majzoob: an incarnate soul that has transcended the finite ego and merged in a state of God-consciousness, but cannot help others*

The Simurgh

As an American approaching Turkish literature for the first time, I relied heavily on Samet Kose for help understanding Turkish culture, the Muslim religion, and the imagery Ahmet employs in his poetry. Chief among the images I needed to understand was one from the title, one selected by Samet as he chose the particular poems from Ahmet's books that he wished to translate for this collection: the simurgh.

An initial search turned up the meaning of a creature something like a griffin or a phoenix that is mostly a fierce bird, sometimes combined with features of a lion or a dog or even with a human face. It is divine and good and giving. Sometimes it appears as a female that can suckle her young. The simurgh is ancient; it is a part of middle eastern culture that predates Islam.

Now, however, Sufi mysticism borrows the image to describe a quality of religion, one which is important to Ahmet's poetry and one which Samet taught me with a legend slightly different than one I found. The legend I found told of a group of thirty birds which travel to find the mythical simurgh. When they arrive, they find only a lake that shows them their reflection. The birds all have a divine quality within them that they can see only when they are searching for the divine. Each bird must strive hard to see God; each must look for himself.

But the legend Samet shared tells a different story. In this legend, a group of birds travel to Mount Qaf, which, like Ultima Thule in Western tradition, is the farthest place anyone can go, the farthest place that exists. This is where the simurgh lives, far away from everyone. As the birds travel to seek the simurgh's advice, they falter and fail one by one until finally, only one bird is left. When this bird arrives, it finds Mount Qaf empty. No simurgh exists. The lone bird concludes that the group of birds that began the journey is the simurgh.

The story seems to say that the divine belongs to all of us, even those of us who fail to search earnestly. The lone bird who arrives, like the legendary simurgh, views the lapsed travelers benevolently. It does not lord its position over them; it shares divinity with them, viewing them as equals — equals necessary to its own divinity.

When Ahmet looks at the world, he looks from the top of a poetic mountain, and he sees God in small places everywhere in the everyday world. But his vision does not fill him with pride. Like the lone bird who arrives, he turns to the rest of the birds and says, "Look how close God is to all of us. Here he is, and here and here. We do not need to travel to the end of the world. To see him, we only need to look at one another with kindness and compassion, and look at the world with gratitude and wonder."

I cannot think of a better message for a book of poetry.

SHARILYN GRAYSON
JULY 4, 2017

An Interview with Ahmet Murat

Samet Kose: Why poetry? When did you start writing poems? What did you write about in the beginning? What provided your first inspiration?

Ahmet Murat: I started my journey with reading poems rather than writing them. While reading a lot of poems, I found my answers deep down about why I loved poetry. I have read so many so that I can find an unwritten one. Then, I decided to write the poems I like to read. Events evolved. In my high school years, I started writing. My very first poem was published in a literature journal. It gave me tremendous courage. I was getting encouraging letters from the editors. I was writing lyric poems. I still preserve that lyrical vein. However, in time that lyrical vein mixed with my sense of humor and irony. You can say these are the essential components of my poetry.

Samet Kose: Place plays an important role in your writing, especially the places you have lived and the places that hold your roots. Tell me about the places that have been important to you. Tell me about Jerusalem and Masjid Aksa.

Ahmet Murat: When I was a child, we had an apple orchard. Hundreds of trees. I was there with my dad to do gardening. I started to realize myself as an extension of nature. I was like a "farmer saint." This exposure educated me in leaves, bugs, worms, apples, clouds, and the ground. While writing poems, I benefited from all the education I received in the orchard. I was in an orchard in a small town in the middle of Turkey and lucky to have a father who was a former military officer, had studied economics, engaged in horticulture, and worked as a merchant at the same time. Now I am forty-some years old and yet can't escape a period I left behind thirty years ago because of such great memories. I've always loved the cities of the East. Jerusalem is one of them. That's where I discovered the stone. From that stone reeks holiness. I swear I have witnessed it. I've lived in Cairo for two years. They're my best years. Don't forget Lahore as well. Sometimes when I am extremely busy, I remember Lahore's noisy, reddish, dusty sky. Fez (the second largest city of Morocco) and Isfahan (the capital of Isfahan Province in Iran) left deep scars inside me. Some cities from Africa, Djibouti, especially South African cities. I can't choose one above another.

Samet Kose: Do you consider yourself a storyteller?

Ahmet Murat: For many years I tried to silence the storyteller inside me, the essayist inside me, and the academic scholar inside me. These forms sounded like cheating poetry to me. But over the years, I think I managed to develop a balance. Now, I can say I founded a guest house within myself where one does not push another.

Samet Kose: Who are your favorite poets to read? Are there books you return to again and again?

Ahmet Murat: Chronologically I can say Sezai Karakoç, Turgut Uyar, Ülkü Tamer, Ahmet Muhip Dıranas, Behcet Necatigil, İsmet Özel, nd Osman Konuk. This is my A-list of poets.

Samet Kose: Poetry is a form of conversation, is it not?

Ahmet Murat: Conversation with a new vocabulary, with a new grammar. Conversation with stuttering and staggering. Conversation like injecting a vaccine at the root of the tongue. The language unfolds, ferments, and turns into a new language.

Samet Kose: In your poems, sometimes we come across words even the Turkish Language Institution's dictionaries seem to be inadequate to define. Could you further elaborate the meaning of resurrecting old forgotten words?

Ahmet Murat: I may have made up some of those words. I extracted some of them from the lexicon of my grandmothers and grandfathers. I used some of them as a building block to complement the sound and music of the poem. But let me tell you something; when I was using those words, it was never a calculated choice. I mean I have never used a word that I had put aside to use later on in another poem. When inspiration sent me assistance, I took the shot. Sometimes the ball hit the back of the net for a perfect goal, sometimes not. But each of them happened at that precious moment, blossomed inside me, arose while I wrote the poem, and made me like them.

Samet Kose: Could you please help me understand the relationship of your poetry to the heritage of this fertile land, this region as a poet of the Near East and Urumeli?

Ahmet Murat: My poems go along well with ancient Arabic songs, Persian timbre, and bozlak. I'm in love with Turkish, admire Arabic, and am a prisoner of Persian. I find myself the soulmate of Galib Dede, the relative of Hafiz, and a kinsman of Shushtari. I guess if my poetry were translated into Eastern languages, for the most part, they would be very familiar to the readers.

Samet Kose: For centuries, Arab poets used "kalb/heart" to signify grace. What does "kalb" signify in your poetry?

Ahmet Murat: "Kalb/heart" signifies purity, simplicity, and the epicenter of childhood. As long as we do not contaminate this sacred place, we can listen to what it says. If someone does not distort the primal nature of the heart, one day he may end up being a nice, virtuous, and sacred man.

Samet Kose: Do you think of yourself/your poetry as political?

Ahmet Murat: My poems cannot directly be considered political. I do not write anything political. But the poetry itself is essentially a political stand. It is political in a sense of breaking through the language and extracting a new language and in directly intervening in the habits in our everyday lives. Poetry is a great form of education. A good poetry reader is analytical, and he hardly ever falls into a trap. This keeps him in a political position.

Samet Kose: Does pain have any dialect? How do people deal with immeasurable losses and tragedies in their lives?

Ahmet Murat: I wrote lyric poems; I still write. You know, every pain and sorrow in our land penetrates everything around us. We're used to living with them. Our folk songs are extremely poignant. The people who write those lyrics have burn scars in their hearts. Every single one of them has a burned lung from sadness. We in the Middle East are from the land of sufferings and losses. Therefore we are fatalistic, rather than absolutely determinist. It would be impossible for us to forget our God. This also gives us strength.

Samet Kose: Another feature of your poems is that they can be read out loud. They are quiet poems but must be read out loud to understand the relationship between the eye and ear. Could you please share their story?

Ahmet Murat: I've always been interested in music in my poetry. For that reason, I read my poems out loud before publishing them. Even if when I don't, I hear my own voice inside me. I construct the sound and rhythm of my poems based on that voice. I want readers to hear that voice as well while reading them.

Samet Kose: Your poems seem to be a record of an essentially lost or forgotten world, the Middle East. Everyone lives life in a language, in a given language; everyone's experiences therefore are heard, absorbed, and recalled in that language. How could you manage to produce the narrative of one language in a different language?

Ahmet Murat: Language surrounds us in a way that does not allow universality. This is the border which makes translation almost impossible. However, reasoning allows us to travel within the borders of universal values, fences of liking, and models of perception. For this reason, in order to translate poetry and literature, one should have a sense of aesthetics in addition to being fluent in both languages like you. We earthlings share the same troubles and have similar scars. See, this stimulates our curiosity for poets and their poems no matter what languages they were written in. But that representation and transition can only be accomplished by competent translators.

Samet Kose: Along with language, geography - especially in the displaced form of departures, arrivals, farewells, exile, nostalgia, homesickness, and belonging — lie at the core of your poems. This memoir somehow forms a bridge between time and place, especially remote time, experiences, and feelings, somehow forming a connection between hearts. Both as narrator and as character, you also consciously do not spare yourself the same ironies or embarrassing recitals. Thank you for this lovely book, and thank you so much for the interview, Ahmet, my dear friend.

Ahmet Murat: These poems were written in Üsküdar (formerly known as Scutari), Turkey. The idea of someone reading them in the U.S., on a new continent, becoming immersed in them, getting himself or herself a coffee at a cafe and feeling the anguish of a poem in this book sounds insane to me. I hope I do not lose my sanity! Samet, I am deeply grateful to you for your interest in my poems, your sincerity, your generosity, and your kindness.

Ahmet Murat was born in 1971 in Karaman, Turkey. He published his first poems in 1992. He started his college education in Cairo, Egypt and completed it in Istanbul, Turkey. He worked in different professions, including farming, proofreading, editing, teaching, and in the television industry as well. He translated books from Khalil Gibran and Tevfik Al-Hakim into Turkish. When his first book *Kaf and Its Color* was published in 1998, he started attracting attention as a poet of his generation. *Kaf and Its Color* attracted special attention as a thoroughly existential effort that was dense with nature images.

His poetry books that followed explored both the problem of existence and the nature of the sacred. For Ahmet, everything in life is connected to nature and carries hidden archetypes. In his poetry, the moon had a sound, the sky had a voice, and even roses, oleanders, and hyacinths shared a laugh in their everyday rituals. Ahmet interweaves the relationship between life and death with a mystical delicacy.

His second and third books, *The Knowledge of Winter* and *A Poet on a Bike* established Ahmet as a poet who created his own language to employ open yet specific imagery unique to him. His most recent book Verdict of the Heart was published in 2014. With this book, the Turkish Association of Authors awarded him "The Poet of the Year Award."

Ahmet is a syndicated columnist in the *Gerçek Hayat* weekly journal and one of the editors of the *Itibar Poetry and Literature Journal* which is published monthly. He recently compiled his essays in *Kuşlarla Sohbetin Şartları (Terms of Conversations with the Birds)* and was published by Ketebe Publishing House in Istanbul, Turkey where he serves as the editor In chief. Ahmet Murat has a PhD in the fields of Islamic Philosophy and Sufism and has conducted research and published articles in the field of the history and literature of Sufism. He currently teaches as a faculty member at Yalova University in Yalova, Turkey and at Ibn Khaldun University in Istanbul, Turkey.

Samet Kose earned his medical doctor degree in 1989 at Hacettepe University School of Medicine in Ankara, Turkey. He completed his residency in psychiatry at Dokuz Eylul University School of Medicine, Department of Psychiatry in Izmir, Turkey. Dr. Kose completed his Psychiatric Neuroimaging Fellowship at the Center for Advanced Imaging Research Medical University of South Carolina in Charleston.

Samet conducted NIH-funded fMRI studies on social bonding, attachment, parenting behavior, and anxiety disorders and continued his postdoctoral work at Vanderbilt University, then did his US internship and psychiatry residency at the University of Mississippi and University of Texas Medical School at Houston. Samet has expertise in areas of social bonding, attachment, personality correlates of psychiatric disorders, empathy, alexithymia, deception, addiction psychiatry, neuroimaging and brain stimulation therapies in psychiatric disorders. Samet translated several psychiatric scales and validated them in the Turkish culture. Samet received NARSAD's *Young*

Investigator, the *Health Emotions Research Institute Scholars Award* at the *Emotion Symposium* (Top 15 neuroscientist), APA's *Junior Investigators Research Colloquium Award*, TRIPS *(Training Residents in Psychiatry Scholarship) Career Award*, PRITE (Top scorer at Psychiatry Residents in Training Exam) *Award, American Academy of Addiction Psychiatry (AAAP) Award/ Mind Games* 1st Place, *APIRE/Janssen Research Scholar Award, AADPRT International Scholars Award* (Top 3 scholars in the USA), and *Brain Conference Award* (Top 5 neuroscientists in the USA). Samet currently serves as the Editor in Chief of *Psychiatry and Clinical Psychopharmacology* and Academic Editor of *Psychiatry and Behavioral Sciences*.

Samet's earlier pioneering work was cited in Katherine Ellison's book entitled *The Mommy Brain: How Motherhood Makes Us Smarter*. Samet regularly translated poems from E. E. Cummings, Ezra Pound, Robert Frost, Adonis, Kavafis, Pablo Neruda, Federico Garcia Lorca, Naomi Shihab Nye, and David Whyte and wrote in Kitap-lık, Cogito, Hece, Cey Sanat, Kirpi Poetry, and Itibar journals. Samet's *Cummings: Selected Poems* was published by Yapi Kredi Yayinlari, Istanbul, Turkey and has received favorable reviews by the literary critics. Samet's most recent book *T. S. Eliot: Complete Poems (1909-1962)* was published by Everest Publishing House and was awarded the *Turkish Writers Association's 2018 Poetry Translation Award*. Samet currently lives in Franklin, Tennessee with his wife Nurgun, his son Omay, and his cat Messi.

*THEODICY: A NOTE

The term theodicy was coined by German philosopher Gottfried Leibniz in his 1710 work, written in French, Essais de Théodicée sur la Bonté de Dieu, La Liberté de L'homme et L'origine du Mal (Theodicy: Essays on the Goodness of God, the Freedom of Man and the Origin of Evil). The word theodicy derives from the Greek words Theos and dikē. Theos is translated as God and dikē can be translated as either trial or judgment. Hence, theodicy literally means justifying God's will and actions. It means justification of divine goodness and providence in view of the existence of evil.

In the Unbearable Lightness of Being, Milan Kundera explains it as a construct to make God's divine existence more reasonable and understandable. In Islamic thought, most Sunni theologians analyzed theodicy from a metaethical standpoint.

Ash'ari theologians argued that ordinary moral judgments stem from emotion and social convention, which are inadequate to either condemn or justify divine actions. Ash'arites hold that God creates everything, including human actions, but they distinguish creation (khalq) from acquisition (kasb) of actions.

Ibn Sina, analyzed theodicy from a purely ontological standpoint, aiming to prove that God, as the absolutely good First Cause, created a good world. Ibn Sina argued that evil refers to a cause of an entity (such as burning in a fire), to being a quality of another entity, or to its imperfection (such as blindness), in which case it does not exist as an entity.

Fakhr al-Din al-Razi, who represented the mainstream Sunni view, challenged Ibn Sina's analysis and argued that it merely sidesteps the real problem of evil, which is rooted in the human experience of suffering in a world that contains more pain than pleasure.

Sufi theologians such as Ibn Arabi were influenced by the ontological theodicy of Ibn Sina. Ibn Arabi (560/1165), known as "the greatest master" in his Al-Futûbāt al-Makkivvah, argues that evil is non-being. Good (khayr) is that which is positive, useful, profitable, and beautiful. The opposite, sharr, is evil or lack of goodness. Hence, it is non-existence. Good only emerges from good. All good exists. Existence is goodness. Evil results when creatures fail to share in existence. God is unlimited goodness, for no creature is as good as He, and there is nothing in creation like Him.